W9-BZD-696

Eating Up and Diving In

CONTENTS

NATIONAL GEOGRAPHIC Hampton-Brown

School Publishing

Words with ee, ea, ie

Look at each picture. Read the words.

ee   ea
_ie_

Example:

d**ee**r

thr**ee**

l**ea**f

m**ea**l

s**ea**l

pi**e**ce

High Frequency Words
few
food
head
hold
into
once

Key Words

Look at the picture.
Read the sentences.

How could a few tiny fleas eat you?

A Fun Flea Place

1. This fun place fits **into** a case.
2. Lots of fleas **once** played here.
3. Just a **few** of these cases are left.
4. **Hold** a lens to make the fleas look big.
5. But keep your **head** and hands away.
6. You do not want to be flea **food**!

GO! **Phonics Games**

NGReach.com

Blood Suckers

by Deanne W. Kells

leech

Some animals are pests to us.

Are animals ever pests to each other?

tick

flea

Some very little animals
are pests to other animals.
Leeches, ticks, and fleas are three
of them. These tiny pests suck
blood from other animals!

Fleas look like black specks. They can jump. They can live next to an animal's skin.

Mother fleas need lots of blood.
To eat, they bite animals. No animal
wants to be a flea's meal! Fleas
make this cat itch.

dog tick

Ticks eat just one food. That is blood. They hold on to the skin of an animal to feed. That can take days.

deer tick

Ticks sit on plant tips. The tick drops off the plant and lands on the animal.

Some ticks have names like the animals they like most. There are dog ticks and deer ticks.

This leech is filled with blood.

Leeches can live in fresh water, the sea, or on land. Both ends of a leech's body can suck blood.

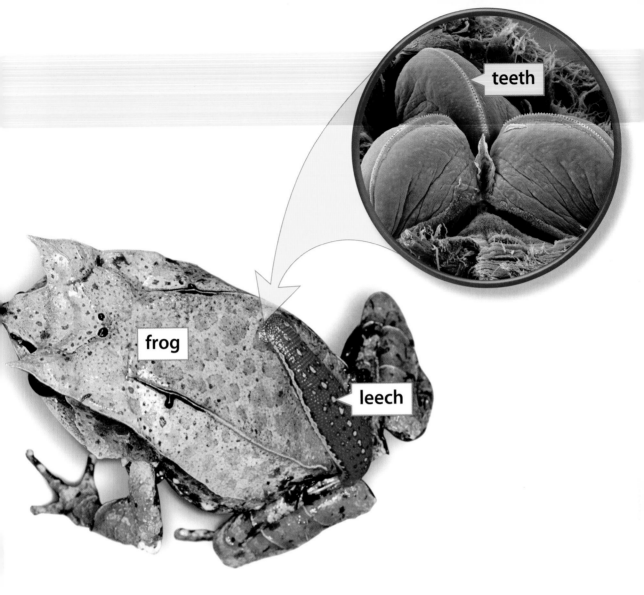

teeth

frog

leech

A leech holds on once it jabs its teeth into an animal. The leech only lets go when it is full. It may not need its next meal for weeks!

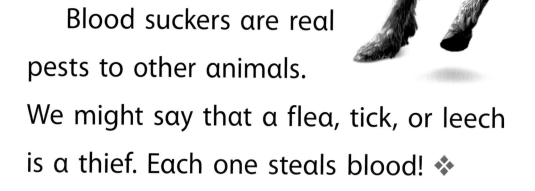

Blood suckers are real
pests to other animals.
We might say that a flea, tick, or leech
is a thief. Each one steals blood! ❖

Words with ee, ea, ie

Read these words.

deer	leech	steer	sweet	wet
flea	mean	strong	thief	

Find the words with
ee, **ea**, and **ie**.
Use letters to build them.

t	h	i	e	f

Talk Together

The ___steer___ looks ___mean___.

Choose words from the box
above to tell your partner
about the animals.

1. deer

2. steer

3. leech

Endings -**ed**, -**ing**

Look at each word pair. Sometimes the first word changes when you add the ending.

fan   fann**ing**

rake   rak**ed**

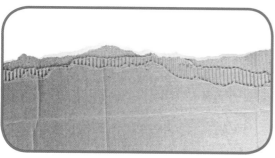

rip   ripp**ed**

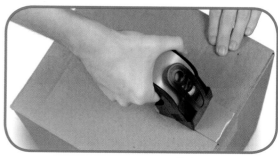

tape   tap**ing**

swim   swimm**ing**

wade   wad**ing**

High Frequency
Words

| few |
| food |
| head |
| hold |
| into |
| once |

Key Words

Look at the picture.
Read the sentences.

Pond Animals

1. You might see just a **few** animals at the pond.
2. **Once** you look for a while, you will see a lot!
3. Look for an animal diving **into** the pond for **food**.
4. You can see just the **head** of one animal.
5. Find the tiny bugs that **hold** on to plants and animals.

What other animals do you see? Find a few.

Phonics Games
NGReach.com

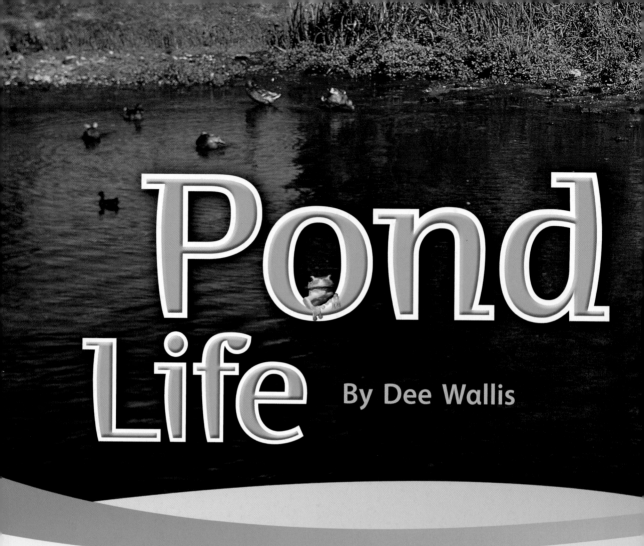

Pond Life

By Dee Wallis

Big and little animals live at a pond. Why do they live there? A pond is filled with food!

Lots of pond animals eat water
plants and bugs. A few eat each other.
Big animals eat little animals like frogs.
And some tiny bugs eat other bugs!

ducks

geese

Ducks and geese eat
water plants.

long neck

swan

webbed feet

These animals have webbed feet.

The webbing helps them move in water.

A swan uses its long neck for reaching

plants under the water.

Some animals live at the edge of a pond. The long legs of a crane work well for wading. This crane has dipped its head into the water to grab a snack.

Frogs lay their eggs in water. Many
frogs are next to water all their lives.
But their long legs are for hopping,
not wading!

Tiny bugs skim on top of a pond to chase food. They eat other bugs by sucking them dry!

Yum!

A turtle is sunning on a log. It just snapped up a bug that tried to fly by!

Under the water, many fish are
swimming. The fish are eating as they are
gliding through the water. The pond is
filled with food for them! ❖

Endings -ed, -ing

Read these words.

feet	legs	spotted	swimming	webbed
hopping	long	strong	wading	

Find the words that end in **-ed** and **-ing**. Use letters to build them.

s p o t t e d

Talk Together

Choose words from the box above to tell your partner about one animal. See if your partner can guess the animal. Take turns.

This animal has long legs for hopping.

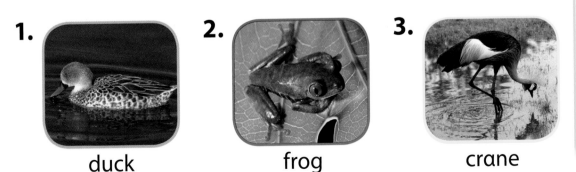

1. duck

2. frog

3. crane

Back to the Pond

Dippy the Duck got lost
in the city. How can he get back to the pond?
Take turns reading the clues with a partner.
Use your finger to trace the way home for Dippy.

1. Look for the big cat head. Take the street
    that leads you to it.

2. Next, look for striped
    cloth. Take the
    street past it.

DEER RANCH

HAIR CUTS

PET SHOP

3. Find a place where you can get a piece of pie for food. Go there.
4. Do you see a place where a few kids are swimming? Go around it.
5. Once you are past it, go into a grassy place.
6. You are at the pond! Dippy has lots of buddies hiding there.

Acknowledgments

Grateful acknowledgment is given to the authors, artists, photographers, museums, publishers, and agents for permission to reprint copyrighted material. Every effort has been made to secure the appropriate permission. If any omissions have been made or if corrections are required, please contact the Publisher.

Photographic Credits

CVR (Cover) Tui De Roy/Minden Pictures. **2** (bl) DigitalStock/Corbis. (br) PhotoDisc/Getty Images. (cl) DigitalStock/Corbis. (cr) PhotoDisc/Getty Images. (tl) Corel. (tr) Philip Lange/iStockphoto. **3** (l) Walt Noon. (r) Liz Garza Williams/Hampton-Brown/National Geographic School Publishing. **4** Thomas Marent/Minden Pictures. **5** (l) Lev Ezhov/iStockphoto. (r) OSF/Paulo De Oliveira/Animals Animals. **6** (b) Carolina K. Smith,M.D./iStockphoto. (t) Heidi & Hans-Juergen Koch/Minden Pictures. **7** Stefan Klein/iStockphoto. **8** (l) Visuals Unlimited/Corbis. (r) Dan Wilton/iStockphoto. **9** (l) Mark Williams/National Geographic Image Collection. (r) Color-Pic, Inc./Animals Animals. **10** (b) Robert Maier/Animals Animals. (t) Tierbild Okapia/Photo Researchers, Inc.. **11** (l) Paul Freed/Animals Animals. (r) Eye of Science/Photo Researchers, Inc.. **12** (c) Arco Images GmbH/Alamy Images. (l) Larysa Dodz/iStockphoto. (r) Juniors Bildarchiv/Alamy Images. **13** (bc) Cody Johnson/iStockphoto. (bl) PureStock/SuperStock. (br) Mircea BEZERGHEANU/Shutterstock. (t) Liz Garza Williams/Hampton-Brown/National Geographic School Publishing. **14** (bl) Wendy Shiao/iStockphoto. (br) Sven Klaschik/iStockphoto. (cl) Aaron Amat/Shutterstock. (cr) Smileus/Shutterstock. (tl) blickwinkel/Alamy Images. (tr) Zavodskov Anatoliy Nikolaevich/Shutterstock. **15** (b) Liz Garza Williams/Hampton-Brown/National Geographic School Publishing. **16-17** Roger Cracknell 1/classic/Alamy Images. **17** (r) Image Source. **18** (b) dabjola/Shutterstock. (c) Sharon Day/Shutterstock. (t) Lainey Dyer/National Geographic Image Collection. **19** (inset) JasonCordell/iStockphoto. (t) George F. Mobley/National Geographic Image Collection. **20** (inset) Janine Bolliger/iStockphoto. **20-21** JillKyle/iStockphoto. **21** (inset) Joe McDonald/Getty Images. **22** (inset) optimarc/Shutterstock. **22-23** Oxilierer/iStockphoto. **23** (b) Artville. (inset) Chas/Shutterstock. **24** Ned M. Seidler/National Geographic Image Collection. **25** (bc) Creatas/Jupiterimages. (bl) Corel. (br) Werner Münzker/iStockphoto. (t) Liz Garza Williams/Hampton-Brown/National Geographic School Publishing.

Illustrator Credits

15 Linda Bittner. **26-27** Peter Grosshauser

The National Geographic Society

John M. Fahey, Jr., President & Chief Executive Officer
Gilbert M. Grosvenor, Chairman of the Board

National Geographic School Publishing
Hampton-Brown
www.NGSP.com

Printed in the USA.
RR Donnelley, Jefferson City, MO

ISBN: 978-0-7362-8041-9

12 13 14 15 16 17 18 19
10 9 8 7 6 5 4

New High Frequency Words

few
food
head
hold
into
once

Target Sound/Spellings

Vowel Digraphs ee, ea, ie	Endings -ed, -ing
Selection: Blood Suckers	**Selection: Pond Life**
deer	filled
each	gliding
eat	hopping
feed	snapped
flea(s)	sunning
leech(es)	swimming
meal	tried
need	wading
real	
sea	
steals	
teeth	
thief	
three	
weeks	